FROM BEAN TO PERFECT CUP
& EVERYTHING IN BETWEEN

New York · Paris · London · Milan

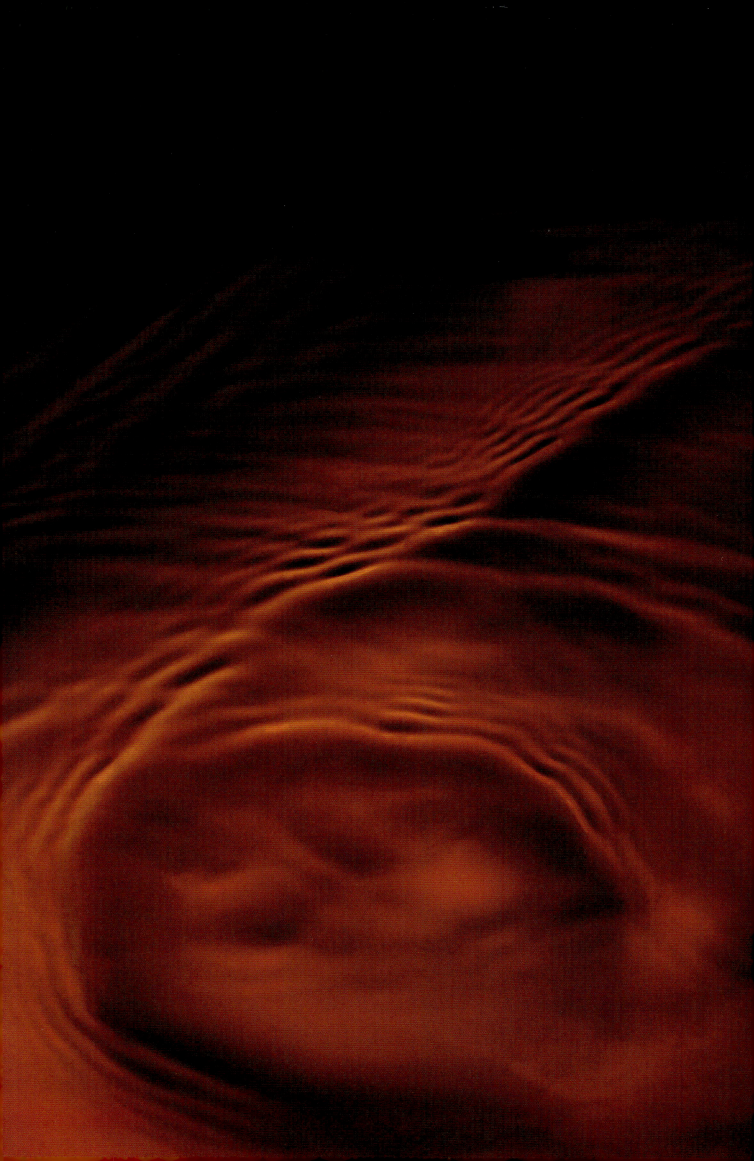

What Do You Really Know about Your Coffee?

There is something about a really good cup of coffee that can be comforting and restorative. Starting with high-quality beans that are grown by farmers who take pride in their work, great coffee is processed, roasted, and ground to deliver a rich, memorable experience.

The stimulating and nurturing effects of coffee have made it a beverage many people cannot live without. Yet it's very easy to take for granted all of the work and numerous steps involved in the process of making the coffee that ends up in our cups.

This book takes a closer look at the craft of coffee making and the many people involved throughout the process. Starting at the farm, we follow the incredible journey of just how much effort and care goes into producing coffee for our enjoyment.

Decades ago, Nespresso understood the importance of precision when brewing coffee and developed a machine that revolutionized coffee making at home. There was no longer a need for the large and very expensive machines found at cafés to enjoy a great cup of coffee. The result was a coffee made at home that could rival a cup from the best cafés in the world.

Since then, the company has scoured the planet to bring consumers the best-tasting coffee available. It has also worked hard to improve farmers' lives and help ensure that farming coffee can be sustainable—both economically and environmentally. In countries such as Colombia, it has worked with farmers to revitalize the coffee industry and help bring fair wages, peace, and stability to areas affected by conflict. The results of these efforts have been profound, with diminished violence around the farms, a new sense of community, and an improved quality of life for the farmers.

Sustainability is integrated into every single aspect of Nespresso's business, from farmer welfare to reforestation, biodiversity, water conservation, LEED-certified roasting plants, and recycling. But it also ensures that the farmers themselves—the people—are sustainable. Without them, we have nothing.

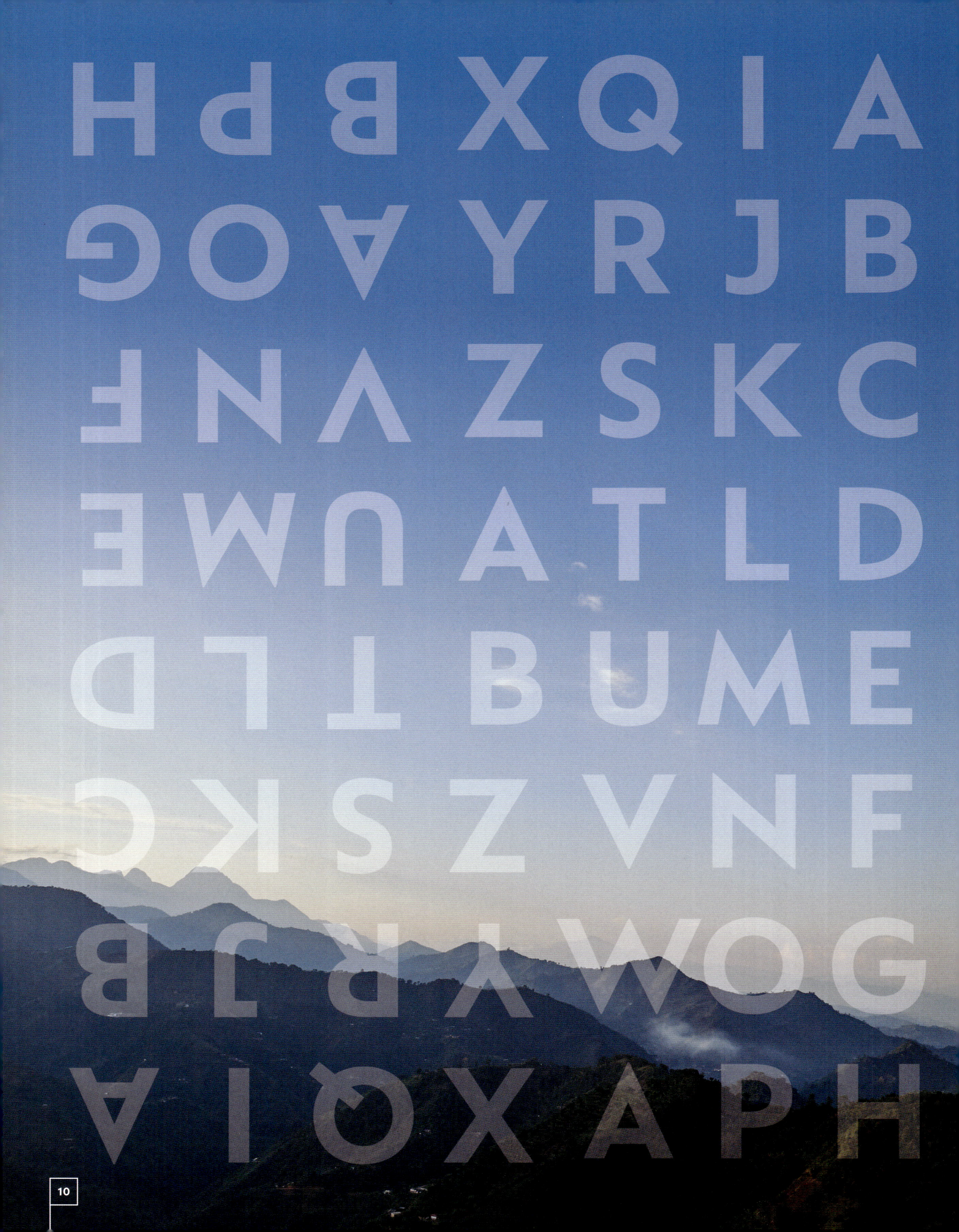

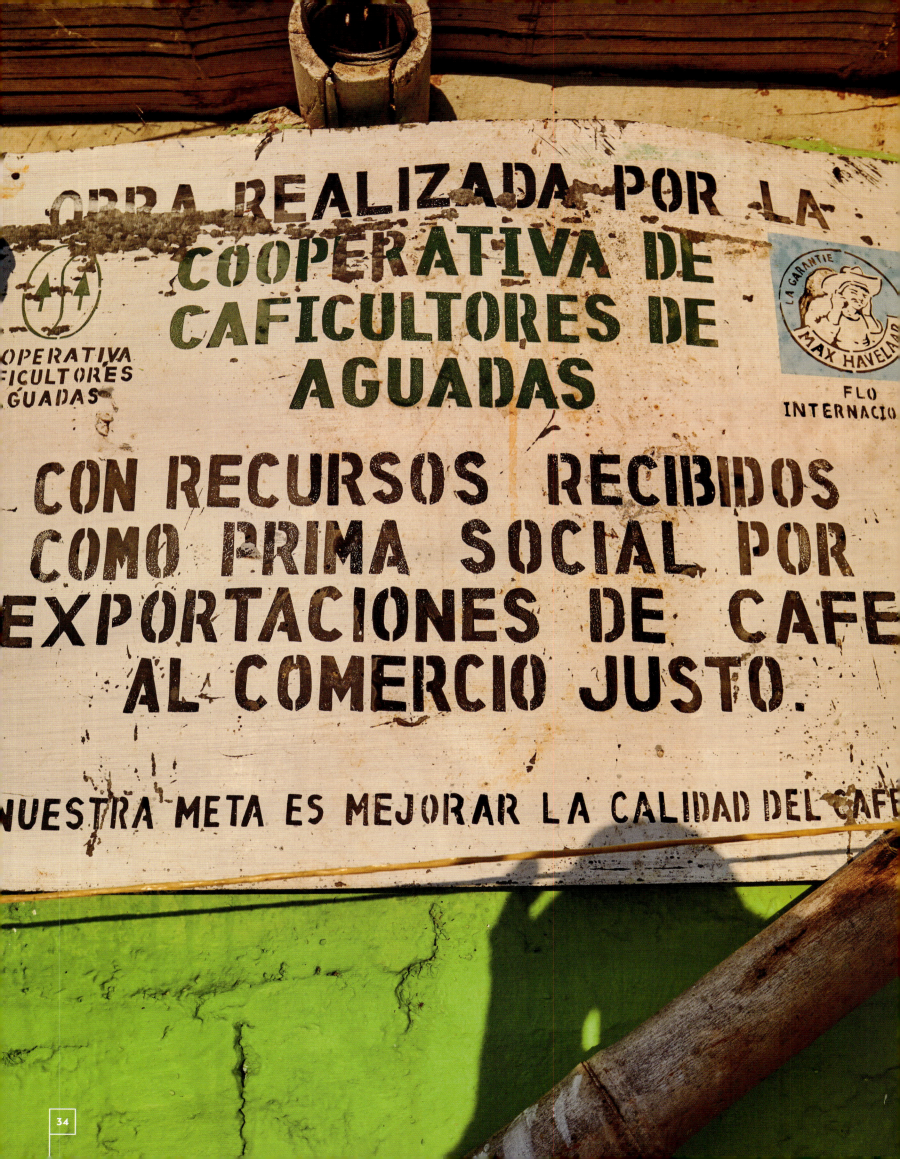

OBRA REALIZADA POR LA
COOPERATIVA DE
CAFICULTORES DE
AGUADAS

COOPERATIVA
CAFICULTORES
AGUADAS

LA GARANTIE
MAX HAVELAAR

FLO
INTERNACIO

CON RECURSOS RECIBIDOS
COMO PRIMA SOCIAL POR
EXPORTACIONES DE CAFE
AL COMERCIO JUSTO.

NUESTRA META ES MEJORAR LA CALIDAD DEL CAFE

(Crema)

The delicate layer of creamy, tiny bubbles floating on the surface of a fine espresso is known as the crema. The crema is often the first indicator of the quality of the espresso itself, and coffee connoisseurs often closely examine it.

The formation of a crema has to do with the intensity of the water pressure as it is being pushed through the coffee grinds and the water's interaction with the oils and carbon dioxide that are released from a fresh grind. The emulsion of the oil and water creates surface tension in the coffee, which encapsulates the aromas that were so carefully created during the roasting process.

The crema is responsible for delivering a sensory profile of aroma and flavor to the nose and back of the mouth as the coffee is first smelled and then tasted. As the silky bubbles rupture, the aromas are further released. The Robusta bean contains natural properties that create a superior crema with thick, uniform bubbles, which is why this bean is often used in espresso blends. A lower-quality crema will dissipate or break up quickly and lay flat, and it can sometimes contain bitter qualities if the beans were over-roasted.

For generations, baristas in Italy and cafés around the world have taken great pride in the art of extracting a perfect cup of espresso with a thick crema on top. To accomplish this, they must ensure that the ground beans are properly packed and the optimal machine water pressure and temperature are maintained. This process produces not only a great-tasting cup of espresso, but also a luxurious, silky crema on top.

By late afternoon, your cherries are pulped. You run the fruit through, placing the sticky seeds into fermentation tanks where they will lie overnight, letting microbes eat away the flesh. The next day, you wash those beans and carefully spread them onto your patio to dry in the sun. Someone in your family will rake them regularly over the next few days so they dry evenly. It's late when you finish your work and return home. Then it's early to bed, resting up for the next day.

Here's the catch: not all cherries on a coffee branch ripen simultaneously, so you have to do this every morning for the couple of months that your coffee is in season. And when that's done, you have no time to rest, because the plants need preparing for the next season. You carefully prune the old wood—a skilled job you won't let anyone else do because it makes all the difference to the next crop. You prune the trees that shelter your coffee from the tropical sun. If you have any money left, you might buy fertilizer to feed your plants or pesticides to fend off the diseases that threaten your crop.

This is the life of a coffee farmer. It is hard and un-forgiving, but filled with the pride of a job well done. The farmers know that if they have done their best, somewhere a roaster might taste their cup and pay a premium for the sweet rewards of their labor. So they are rightfully proud of their efforts, of all the skill and devotion they have lavished on their coffee. This is their land; they have worked it hard and well. Though often humble in nature, they hold their heads high, knowing they have done what not everyone can.

According to Fair Trade, 80 percent of the world's coffee is produced by smallholder farmers who might own only a couple acres of land. If there is a dramatic climate effect, they are vulnerable. If there is an epidemic of pests attacking their coffee, they are vulnerable. If there is a dip in the volatile financial markets against which their coffee price is pegged, they are vulnerable. It's no picnic being a coffee farmer.

At Nespresso, our gratitude to these titans of the value chain is immense. Without them, our business would wither, so it's in our obvious interest to safeguard their futures. In 2003, we created the AAA Sustainable Quality Program to do just that. We focus on quality, because our product needs that; sustainability, because it's not just for now but forever; and productivity, because it does no farmer any good to produce a great coffee in tiny quantities. Farmers need both quality and quantity to earn a decent return. Fifteen years later, more than 75,000 farmers in 12 countries of origin are part of the program, helped by more than 350 agronomists working with them in the field.

(Italy)

We cannot explore the world of coffee without talking about Italy. The country has had a love affair with coffee ever since the beans were first brought into the ports of Venice during the Renaissance. Italian coffee eventually became a cultural phenomenon and part of the social fabric of everyday life.

Italians are responsible for creating the first espresso machine, and for coining the term *espresso*, which is Italian for "expressed" or "forced out." This is precisely how an espresso is made—by forcing pressurized hot water through finely ground and compacted coffee.

La Pavoni Europiccola®

Early evidence of this process was in 1884, when Italian inventor Angelo Moriondo filed a patent for a machine that was designed to force steam and hot water through ground coffee at very high pressure. This machine was a bulk brewer, and at the time it was not designed for individual servings.

Several years later, another Italian, Luigi Bezzera, improved upon Moriondo's design, which helped spur the popularity of espresso in Italy. Bezzera, who was living in Milan at the time, was intrigued with coffee and enhanced the concept by developing a machine that would brew individual espresso drinks.

1884

Angelo Moriondo

The popularity of espresso grew rapidly as coffee bars became part of Italian culture and coffee became an alternative to alcohol as a social lubricant. In the early days of espresso, there was an Italian tax on seating, so frugal customers would instead stand at the bar to sip their beverage. People grew used to enjoying their coffee while standing and engaging in conversation. Coffee culture began to be recognized as a popular way of life within urban areas. Espresso became the predominant coffee beverage; it could be ordered by simply asking for *un caffè*. In Italy today, one can still see Italians enjoying their morning coffee by standing at the bar.

Opposite: The village of Monte Isola on Lake Iseo, Italy

Indonesia Java Jampit

Arabica

Washed

Description: fine et douce acidité, notes de noix (fruits secs)

(Knowledge)

Creating a delicious cup of coffee at home can be a rewarding experience, one in which an understanding of the coffee-making process is important.

It's helpful to learn about equipment, brewing techniques, and the bean's origin and characteristics in order to create a coffee that is right for you. A general understanding of the coffee-producing countries and the types of beans that each region produces can be useful in selecting a flavor profile that appeals to you. What is it that you want in a coffee? Is it an intense or mild flavor? Is it a short or long cup? Do you like citrus or cocoa notes? What sort of aftertaste do you desire?

Selecting the right equipment is a good first step to take at home. Decide if you prefer a fully automatic machine or something more traditional, such as a French press or pour-over. A good-quality coffee grinder and scale are musts for most coffee connoisseurs—and valuable tools to portion and grind just the right amount of coffee.

Experimenting in small batches is key, and tasting a lot of different coffees from different regions is a great way to narrow down what suits you. It's usually best to start on a small scale, brewing and experimenting in small batches while adjusting and changing the brew time, amount of coffee, and coffee region. Take note of the coffee's flavor, intensity level, and whether it's sweet or bitter. Once you find a bean you like, adjusting the brew time and amount of coffee can have a dramatic effect on the final flavor.

Nespresso invites you to visit one of its more than 50 boutique locations in the United States for a free tasting and education from one of our coffee specialists. Here you will be able to taste coffees from around the world and learn about the art of creating a great cup of coffee at home.

(Latte)

The popularity of coffee and espresso around the world has grown exponentially over the past century. Drinking coffee has become part of our culture, something that is integral to our daily routine and lifestyle. Over the years, artisans have developed new recipes to enhance the classic espresso by adding steamed milk and other ingredients. The daily consumption of espresso-based beverages with milk added has nearly tripled in the last decade alone.

The latte is one of these espresso-and-milk beverages, making up the lion's share of popularity. The word latte is short for the Italian term *caffè latte*, meaning "coffee milk." This was something often prepared at home, with the milk warmed in a small pan or moka pot and poured over the espresso. A caffè latte is essentially equal parts steamed milk and espresso, with a very small layer of frothed milk, or foam, at the top.

(Origin)

Merriam-Webster defines the word *origin* first as "ancestry or parentage." In coffee, the word evokes wildly romantic visions of the exotic countries where coffee is grown. Wherever one lies on the spectrum of the coffee experience, origin is that magical, mythical place where it all begins—the soaring, cloud-covered mountains of one's imagination, reached only by long, grueling journeys to remote and disconnected places. Here the farmer produces that sweet little coffee cherry in his tropical, idyllic isolation, supplying the cafés of our connected world.

The reality, however, is much less dreamy and more demanding than this romanticized image. There are days of unrelenting rain, bumpy access roads, slippery and steep mountain paths, basic accommodations, sporadic electricity, and limited Wi-Fi connectivity, but one fact is immutable and true: origin is where it all begins.

Coffee's natural habitat is the world's equatorial belt between the Tropics of Cancer and Capricorn—with few exceptions, no more than 23 degrees off the equator. That is the origin of this delicious, beloved bean.

(Precision)

To create a really great-tasting coffee, precision needs to be part of each step of the coffee-making process. From the handling of the beans, to the systems used to fill the capsules, to the machines that brew the coffee at home—each component is designed to run with the accuracy and precision of a fine watch. With its Swiss roots, Nespresso is devoted to precision. Each movement in its factory is well thought out, perfectly timed, and done with deliberate intention.

Batches of coffee are roasted to perfection using exacting specifications based on the varietal blend and origin. The roasting only happens after the multistep cupping practice confirms the quality of beans and how they compare to the company standard. Not only are there 17 different tastings along the way, but also infrared scanning to ensure there are no flaws in any of the beans. The roasting process is performed by equipment that can heat the beans to the desired temperature and then cool them rapidly within seconds so they are not over-roasted.

The beans are then swiftly transported through a complex system of tubes to the grinding machines. To protect the freshness of the coffee so it doesn't oxygenate, the beans are never exposed to air during this process. The beans are ground four different times to achieve the desired size and shape that Nespresso's coffee experts require for an optimal extraction.

The ground beans are then sent, still via oxygen-free tubing, to the automated stations that fill each aluminum capsule with the precise amount of coffee before they are sealed for freshness and boxed.

Precision at Nespresso also relates to the design and function of its machines for brewing at home. From its humble beginnings more than 30 years ago, the company pioneered single-use capsule machines that are able to deliver consistent results time and time again. Years of engineering went into creating a machine that could brew a high-quality coffee that would exemplify the natural characteristics of the coffee bean. The machines are programmed to push the exact amount of water through the coffee grinds at the precise temperature and pressure.

needed to brew a cup. The third was the capsule. Using enough water and coffee, but not more than you need, becomes a very interesting driver for single serve. Precision is absolutely key. As for the capsule, it is the vehicle used to convey a great cup of coffee from a coffee plant to a cup. And this vehicle can be reused again and again. Then you reach an optimum case where you don't lose anything anymore. You get the precise amount of food or water you need, combined with a reusable packaging. I believe in this recipe. I believe in this equation. That's why we have invested so much in recycling because not recycling would be a missed opportunity to optimize your system. And on top of that, we have consumers eager to engage in this recycling program. Every single month, we see recycling volumes going up and up and up, which is absolutely great, and I thank all of the Nespresso Club members for their support.

Katz: We all have our hands on the chain saws, so we are all responsible. We need to recognize that we thrive and survive along with the coffee farmers, and we need to pay closer attention to the things we use and take for granted on a daily basis. And we think Nespresso understands that and has taken a leadership role.

(Terroir)

You might think we're pompous or jargonistic in using the word *terroir*, but its meaning is core to what is so special about coffee. Think of it like a human being. We are all made of the same essence, but the environment in which we are raised makes all the difference in the end.

The altitude at which coffee grows, the latitude at which it lies, the soil in which it is rooted and that supplies its vital minerals, the rainfall that nourishes it and helps its cherries grow, the sunshine that allows for photosynthesis and so feeds the plant, the position on the mountainside (whether coffee is facing the sun or in the shade)—all of this is terroir. Every little thing in a coffee plant's microclimate shapes the way it develops and ultimately the way its fruit tastes. Of course, it's not only terroir that impacts taste. The plant species and variety, the farmer's cultivation and care, the post-harvest processing method, the shipping time, and the way the bean is roasted all impact the final cup.

But it all begins with terroir. At Nespresso, we look for specific taste profiles to deliver a consistently high-quality cup, so our first step is to find microclimates most likely to produce those profiles. The impact is so decisive that a single coffee plant variety will express itself quite differently in different environments. Take the world-famous Geisha variety, for example, known for its fine jasmine blossom notes. In its genetic homeland in western Ethiopia, it grew nearly 6,000 feet above sea level. In the middle of the 20th century, it was

Vietnam   *India*

disseminated in Central America and eventually planted in many coffee-growing regions. But it was not until it showed its face in Panama toward the end of the century that its prominent floral notes were recognized and rewarded. It needed that altitude to best express its personality—and that did not happen at lower-altitude farms.

So don't think we are using the French word gratuitously; we're using it because it makes all the difference in the world to how good our coffee tastes.

Ethiopia   *Colombia*

A conversation between an Ethiopian farmer and an agronomist about the new crop of coffee

Young adults also appreciate artisan-made products and put a lot of value on items that are handcrafted and sourced or processed locally. They also develop interpersonal relationships with the makers, and, in the case of coffee, the roasters or baristas. This young generation is respectful and appreciative of an artisan who has learned to master a specific craft and hold that person in high regard.

Young adults continue to lead the way in shaping products brought to market and have been successful in steering businesses to adjust practices and policies based on their beliefs. As their voices increase, there is no doubt that the values and ideas of today's young people will be heard.

Opposite: An Indian coffee farmer sharing his recent discoveries about a new variety with a technician

(Zealot)

The love affair with coffee seems to grow with each passing year and, not surprisingly, coffee is more popular than beer, wine, or hard liquor. Coffee enthusiasts, or zealots, are deeply passionate about their coffee and acutely aware of where it was grown, how it was roasted, and its proper brewing technique. They are experts in evaluating the coffee's bitterness or sweetness, level of acidity, and the subtle notes evident in the liquid and fine crema.

But not so long ago, coffee in the United States was typically of low quality and often purchased in cans at a supermarket or consumed at a diner. It had an unremarkable taste and an unknown origin. Over time, small independent coffee roasters and coffeehouses began to change the consumer's perception of coffee. Coffeehouses had existed in Europe for centuries, but did not become popular in the United States until the 1950s and 1960s. Suddenly, coffees from Kenya, Ethiopia, Brazil, India, and other regions became more widely available and their distinctive flavor profiles were embraced by a new generation of coffee drinkers.

Knowledge was a key element that transformed consumers' interest in coffee. Their tastes began to evolve, and they began to seek out these high-quality, specialized coffees that were previously not widely available. This helped propel the phenomenon of "coffeehouse culture," further popularizing the beverage and allowing it to become part of a lifestyle. It's not uncommon to hear someone say, "I can't think until I have my first cup of coffee," or "I can't function without coffee." And although these may seem like exaggerations, the feelings and opinions about this beverage are quite strong.

Consumers have become more interested in the journey of the coffee they drink. Zealots know what region their coffee comes from and who farms it. They are aware of the area's terroir and what factors contribute to the flavor and aroma profiles. Whether they are enjoying their coffee at home or at a coffeehouse, chances are the zealots are fully aware of their coffee's entire journey from bean to cup.

Coffee has become such a vital part of the human diet—not only as a hot beverage, but as a cold beverage, cocktail, ingredient in savory cooking, and a pairing item in gourmet meals. In the following pages, Nespresso shares some of its favorite recipes. Enjoy!

PEPPERMINT WHITE
CHOCOLATE LATTE

INGREDIENTS

• 2 capsules of Decaffeinato Intenso or

Arpeggio Decaffeinato

• ¾ ounces peppermint syrup

• 1 ounce white chocolate sauce + extra for garnish

• 5 ounces milk

• Whipped cream (for garnish)

• Crushed peppermint candies (for garnish)

DIRECTIONS

• In a mug, mix peppermint syrup and white
  chocolate sauce.

• Froth milk and add to mug.

• Brew capsules directly over frothed milk and
  stir to combine.

• Top with whipped cream, additional white
chocolate sauce, and peppermint candies.